Jack Johnson

Nick Healy

Raintree

Chicago, Illinois

© 2003 Raintree
Published by Raintree, a division of Reed Elsevier, Inc.
Chicago, Illinois
Customer Service 888-363-4266
Visit our website at www.raintreelibrary.com

For information, address the publisher
Raintree, 100 N. LaSalle, Suite 1200, Chicago, IL 60602

Printed and bound in the Unites States at Lake Book Manufacturing, Inc.
07 06 05 04 03
10 9 8 7 6 5 4 3 2 1

Library of Congress Cataloging-in-Publication Data

Healy, Nick.
  Jack Johnson / Nick Healy.
    v. cm. -- (African American biographies)
  Includes bibliographical references and index.
  Contents: Growing up in Galveston -- Rising in the ranks -- Crossing the color line -- The great white hope -- Challenges for the champ -- Coming home -- Johnson's place in history.
    ISBN 07398-6873-X (HC), 1-4109-0036-3 (Pbk.)
  1. Johnson, Jack, 1878-1946--Juvenile literature. 2. Boxers (Sports)--United States--Biography--Juvenile literature. 3. African American boxers--Biography--Juvenile literature. [1. Johnson, Jack, 1878-1946. 2. Boxers (Sports) 3. African Americans--Biography.] I. Title. II. Series: African American biographies (Chicago, Ill.)

GV1132.J7H43 2003
796.82'092--dc21
                              2002153812

Acknowledgments
The publishers would like to thank the following for permission to reproduce photographs:
pp. 4, 6, 14, 17, 22, 24, 26, 28, 30, 33, 36, 38, 41, 44, 51, 54, 58 Bettmann/CORBIS; pp. 8, 49 Hulton/Archive by Getty Images; pp. 10, 12, 35, 46, 57 CORBIS; pp. 21, 52 Hulton-Deutsch Collection/CORBIS.

Cover photograph: Bettmann/CORBIS

Content Consultant
C. Keith Harrison, Ed.D., Assistant Professor
Director, The Paul Robeson Research Center for Academic and Athletic Prowess Kinesiology-SMC
The University of Michigan
Ann Arbor, Michigan 48109-2214

Some words are shown in bold, **like this.** You can find out what they mean by looking in the Glossary.

Contents

Jack Johnson fought racial prejudice to become the first African American to be the World Heavyweight Boxing Champion.

Introduction

Jack Johnson did the impossible and made it look easy. He began life as a child in a Texas city that was rough and poor. He left school and went to work at a very young age. There did not seem to be a lot of opportunity for him in life. Yet he was determined to do great things, and he succeeded. Johnson became the first African American to be **heavyweight** champion in boxing, and he was famous around the world. (Boxers are put into groups by how much they weigh. Heavyweight is the term used for the group that weighs the most.)

His accomplishments seemed impossible for many reasons. Johnson was a timid child who was picked on by schoolmates. He learned most of his boxing skills on his own. Most experts figured he could not hold up against the champions of that time. Nearly everyone agreed that he would never get the chance anyway. After all, Johnson was an African American, and only whites were allowed to compete for the championship.

This fight between Jack Johnson and Jim Jeffries, that took place on July 4, 1910, was called "The Fight of the Century."

But Johnson was determined to reach his goal. He boxed for more than ten years and showed that he was the best African-American boxer. His personality and style also made him famous. Some people loved him. Others did not like him at all. But everyone had to agree that he was a great fighter. Johnson finally got his chance against the white man who was **heavyweight** champion in 1908. Johnson won that match and stayed champion for seven years.

Johnson's name is not well known now, but his fame lives on in sports. He was a hero to later boxing champions such as Muhammad Ali (see page 52). He also opened the door for African Americans to compete in boxing, baseball, and other professional sports.

In His Own Words

"If I felt any better, I'd be scared myself."

Talking before the Tommy Burns championship fight in 1908

"I want to say that I am not a slave and that I have a right to choose who my mate shall be."

Responding to uproar over his marriage to a white woman

Arthur John Johnson, known as Jack, was born March 31, 1878, in Galveston, Texas.

Chapter 1:
The First Years

Fame seemed unlikely for the third child born to Henry Johnson and his wife, Tiny. Their son was born March 31, 1878. His full name was Arthur John Johnson, but he was known by the nickname Jack. The family lived in Galveston, Texas. It was a place where people worked very hard to get by financially.

Henry Johnson had been born as a slave in Maryland. When he was young, Henry had boxed against other slaves. They fought with bare knuckles in those days. It was a dangerous game meant to entertain the wealthy landowners. If Henry received any rewards for his boxing, they were very small.

Some slaves were freed before or during the Civil War. Most of them lived in the North. After the war ended in 1865, all slaves, including Henry, were freed. A free man, Henry made his way to Galveston, a city near the Gulf of Mexico. It was the largest city in

Thousands of freed slaves like these on the USS Vermont *worked on ships for the United States Navy during the Civil War.*

Texas. Ships carried goods in and out from the docks in Galveston. Many slaves like Henry had never been taught to read or write. Once freed, they often took jobs that included a lot of hard work. Loading and unloading ships was one way for people like Henry to make a living. That made a place like Galveston appeal to former slaves.

Henry held several different jobs in his first years in Texas. Soon he became the janitor at the local school for African-

American students. He stayed in that job for more than 10 years. He used his pay to buy a small piece of land in Galveston. He built a small house on that land. Owning land and a home was a major accomplishment for a former slave.

Henry Johnson married a woman named Tiny, and they started a family. Their first child was born in 1872. It was a girl they named Lucy. Next was a daughter named Jennie. Jack was the third child. He was followed by Henry, Fannie, and Charles.

Separate Schools

The school where Henry worked was for African-American students only. There were separate schools for African-American children and white children in Texas and many other states at the time. The schools were separate because of something called **segregation.** Segregation is a set of rules that forces the races to live apart from each other. Today segregation is not legal. Laws demand that all people be treated equally.

In Johnson's day, schools were just one place where segregation was enforced. In some places, African Americans were forced to eat in separate restaurants. They had to stay in separate hotels. They even drank from separate drinking fountains. Some shops would hang signs that said "whites only" in the window. That kind of separation was also used in sports. Jack Johnson found out later how hard it was to overcome segregation.

This outhouse at a Greyhound bus station in Louisville, Kentucky, in 1943 shows how African Americans were unfairly treated in the United States under the rules of segregation.

School Days

Henry and Tiny Johnson believed education was very important. They wanted their children to learn to read and write. They made sure their children went to school every day and kept up on schoolwork. Jack Johnson's school days were not always happy. Jack was a smart child, and he did well in class. The problem was that he was picked on by the other children.

Johnson was a tall child, and he was strong. But he was also quiet and timid. He did not like to defend himself when bullies pushed him around. His older sister Lucy often protected him on the playground. She would fight off the children who picked on Jack. Tiny Johnson did not like it. She did not want her son to fight, but she wanted him to defend himself. Johnson began to fight back against the bullies when he had no other choice. He found that he was good at it.

At age 12, Jack Johnson left school. He was old enough that he was expected to work and help the family. Many children, no matter what color they were, had to leave school after sixth grade in those days because their families were poor and they were old enough to work. Johnson found work on the docks and anywhere else he could get it. In his free time, he practiced the sport that would make him famous. He lifted weights, jumped rope, and hit the punching bag. He boxed in practice matches. He learned how to be a better fighter.

Jack Johnson practices boxing with a fellow fighter, Floyd Patterson, in 1922. Johnson helped train Patterson, who later became an Olympic and World Heavyweight Champion.

Chapter 2:
Rising in the Ranks

In Jack Johnson's time, it was not easy for a young man to become a professional boxer. That was especially true if the young man was an African American. There was no place for him to sign up for lessons. He had to learn the hard way.

As a teenager, Johnson realized he could be a good boxer. He was stronger than other boys his age. He was quick on his feet. He could dodge a punch. He could throw one so fast that no opponent could dodge it.

To prove his skills, Johnson had to take part in fights known as battle royals. These were dangerous events held on the streets of Galveston and other cities. In a battle royal, a group of young men would all fight each other. The fights were set up by white men. They were meant to entertain gamblers. They were similar to the fights Johnson's father had been in when he was a slave.

Sometimes the battle would begin with fifteen or more young men involved. It was every man for himself. The last person on his feet would win pennies and nickels thrown from the crowd.

Johnson often won. Sometimes the other fighters would join together to try to beat him, but he still found a way to win. He made a name for himself that way. He was soon able to leave the battle royals behind.

A Start in Boxing

Johnson needed more than a tough reputation to get a chance in boxing. He had to show that he was ready for a real match. To prove himself, Johnson was a **sparring** partner for the best boxers in Galveston. A sparring partner is someone whom a professional boxer fights for practice. Johnson moved from city to city to get work as a sparring partner. He went to Boston and worked for a talented fighter named Joe Walcott. Walcott saw that Johnson could be great. He encouraged Johnson and coached him during their workouts.

Johnson's first professional boxing match was in 1897. He was just 19 years old at the time. He faced a Galveston boxer named Jim Rocks. Johnson knocked Rocks out in the fourth round. The small crowd saw a hint of the skill that Johnson would later show the whole world.

Joe Walcott demonstrates his uppercut for the camera. Walcott was one of Johnson's sparring partners before Johnson became a professional boxer.

A Hard Lesson

Johnson's march toward boxing fame moved slowly at first. He fought only once more in 1897 and won again. He was in three matches the next year. He won all except one, which was declared a **draw**. A draw is a tie in boxing. It means neither boxer has won.

Johnson's first loss in the ring came in 1899. He had gone to Chicago to fight Klondike Haynes. Haynes was one of the better African-American fighters of the time. It was hard to know how African-American boxers compared to white boxers in those days. African Americans did not get to fight white boxers often, and no African American had been given a chance against the white champ.

Johnson's loss to Haynes was unusual. Johnson did well in the first few rounds, but he tired quickly. Johnson could not go on in the fifth round. He quit, and Haynes was the winner. Johnson learned that he needed to practice hard and get into great shape. Otherwise, he could not last against the best.

Toward a Title

After his first loss, Johnson was determined to prove himself. He fought Klondike Haynes again later that year. The match ended in frustration for Johnson. Haynes and Johnson fought for twenty **rounds**. Back then, a round lasted three minutes, with one minute for the boxers to rest between rounds. The fight was ruled a draw.

Johnson needed to beat Haynes to prove that he was one of the top boxers. Johnson kept working on his moves and got another chance several months later. Finally, Johnson got the best of Haynes. In the 14th round, Johnson knocked him out.

That win was the start of something big. Johnson soon left Texas and went to California. That was where most of the best African-American boxers could be found. It was also where he could win the separate championship for African Americans. The separate title was called the Colored **Heavyweight** Championship.

Facing a Famous Name

People in California knew little about Johnson when he first arrived. He changed that quickly. Johnson was in 13 matches in 1902. He had 10 victories and three draws. He beat some of the most famous African-American fighters of the time. Johnson gained the respect of people who followed boxing.

Jack Johnson also beat a white boxer that year. He was matched against Jack Jeffries, who was the older brother of the white heavyweight champion, Jim Jeffries. Many people said Jim Jeffries was the best boxer of any race. His brother Jack was not nearly as good. African Americans and whites did box against each other back then. However, **segregation** stopped African Americans from getting a chance at the championship. Johnson dominated the match from the beginning. In the fifth **round,** Johnson knocked out Jack Jeffries. His brother, the champ, watched from the front row.

A Separate Championship

The next step for Johnson was to win the Colored **Heavyweight** Championship. He got his chance early in 1903. He was ready for it. More than 4,000 fans gathered in Los Angeles to see the match. Johnson's opponent was called Denver Ed Martin. He was bigger than Johnson and looked like the stronger man. The fight started slowly. Martin was more **aggressive** in the early rounds. He went after Johnson and threw many more punches.

The action changed in the 11th round. Martin had grown tired by then, and Johnson knew it. He went after Martin with bigger and harder blows. Johnson knocked Martin down three times in that round. Martin somehow managed to get through the rest of that match. But the winner was clear after 20 rounds of action. The referee raised Johnson's hand to announce his victory.

Jack Johnson, at about age 22, ready to fight, stands with his hands low, trying to get his opponent to take a swing.

Johnson stayed in shape for boxing by running often. He is shown here running with his trainer in 1915.

Chapter 3:
Crossing the Color Line

Jack Johnson wanted to take on the white champion. Everyone agreed he was a **contender**. A contender is a boxer who is one of the 10 best in his weight group. However, something was in his way. That thing was going to be harder to beat than any boxer Johnson had ever seen. It was called the **color line**.

The color line was part of **segregation.** It was an imaginary border that African Americans and other people of color could not cross. The color line kept many African-American athletes out of professional sports. For example, no African Americans were allowed to play professional baseball in the early 1900s. That did not change until 1947.

In 1903, Johnson had no example to follow. He was going to have to be the first to cross the color line in a major sport.

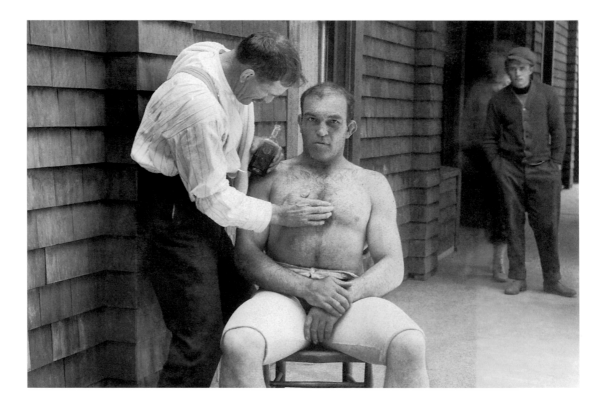

Jim Jeffries, seated here as his trainer rubs oil onto his chest so that punches slide off it, was the World Heavyweight Champion from 1899 to 1905.

Challenging the Champ

Johnson said he wanted to fight the white champion. Newspapers around the country reported the challenge. Many boxing fans hoped the fight would happen. Jim Jeffries was still the heavyweight champion at the time. He did not accept Johnson's challenge.

In 1904, Johnson and Jeffries just happened to be in the same saloon in San Francisco. Johnson talked to Jeffries face to face. He again challenged Jeffries to give him a chance at the championship. Jeffries said no, but he had a challenge for Johnson.

Jeffries suggested they go down in the cellar and fight. Jeffries wanted to make a bet of $2,500 with Johnson. The winner of the fight would get the money. The title of world champion would not be on the line.

Johnson said he was a boxer, not a cellar fighter. Johnson said he wanted to be treated the same as a white challenger. He wanted a fair fight for the championship. The two left the saloon and did not meet again for several years.

Later that year, Jeffries decided to quit boxing. He retired as champion. He had never been beaten. He had never even been knocked down by an opponent. It looked like Johnson would never have the chance to fight the great champ.

Waiting for a Chance

Johnson spent the next few years making a name for himself. He remained the Colored Heavyweight Champion and beat the best African-American challengers. He also took on white heavyweights who were willing to face him. The **color line** did not prevent whites from boxing African Americans. Only championship fights were off limits to African Americans.

Sports writers often wrote negative things about Tommy Burns, seen here punching a bag as part of his training, because he was willing to fight African Americans.

From 1905 to 1907, Johnson boxed often and usually won easily. He went all over the United States to take on the top boxers in many cities. Sometimes he even had two matches on the same day. He could not get a chance at the championship, but he could earn plenty of money by winning lots of matches.

Things began to change in 1907. Boxing was losing fans and needed something to excite people. The white heavyweight champion was a man named Tommy Burns. He was a good boxer, but was not a famous champ like Jeffries had been. Many fans realized that Johnson was the best **heavyweight** in the sport. It was getting harder to ignore Johnson.

Boxing was also in trouble in another way. Some leaders in government and in churches were against boxing. They thought it was too violent and dangerous. They wanted the sport to be outlawed. Indeed, boxing was banned in some cities and states at the time.

The Big Fight

In 1908, Johnson was finally allowed to cross the **color line.** Tommy Burns agreed to a match against Johnson. The fight was scheduled for the day after Christmas that year. A stadium in Sydney, Australia, was chosen for the location. The match was in Australia to avoid the problems of **segregation** in the United States.

Disaster Hits Galveston

In 1900, Jack Johnson's hometown was destroyed by a terrible disaster. Galveston, Texas, sits on the shore of the Gulf of Mexico. Hurricanes move in from the gulf and bring high winds, rain, and flood waters. The storm that hit Galveston in 1900 was the worst ever seen in the United States.

The hurricane hit the city on September 8. The winds roared at more than 110 miles per hour (177 kilometers per hour). Homes and businesses were blown over. Wood, glass, and other materials filled the air and injured many people. Six thousand people were killed by the storm. Thousands of others lost their homes and everything they owned. The house that Johnson's father had worked so hard to build was flattened.

There are many reasons that Johnson was allowed to cross the color line. One of the biggest reasons was money. The **promoters** knew the match would get the attention of the entire world. Promoters are people who organize boxing matches. They sell the tickets to the public and pay the fighters when the match is over. The promoters knew lots of people would want to see the white champ against the African-American champ.

The promoters were right. A crowd of 20,000 people jammed into the Sydney stadium to see the match. In other countries, people crowded outside newspaper offices to wait for reports from Australia. There was no radio or television at that time.

Burns was a Canadian who was known for being tough and **aggressive.** He was not a big man for a heavyweight boxer. He was just 5 feet, 7 inches tall and weighed 170 pounds. Johnson was taller than 6 feet and weighed more than 190 pounds. Still, many white fans expected Burns to win easily. They did not think an African American could hold up against a white champion.

Those fans were in for a surprise. Johnson was in charge from the start of the match. He knocked Burns down in the first round, but Burns got up quickly and kept fighting.

In round after round, Johnson dodged Burns. Johnson let Burns wear himself out, and then he took charge. He battered Burns in the 12th and 13th round. In the 14th, he knocked Burns down again. Burns got back on his feet, but the fight was over. The police entered the ring to protect Burns. The police thought he would be hurt if the match went any longer. The referee raised Johnson's hand in victory.

It was December 26, 1908. At last, Johnson was the one and only **heavyweight** champion of the world.

This photo shows Jack Johnson when he was Heavyweight Champion of the World. It was taken sometime between 1908 and 1914.

Chapter 4:
The Great White Hope

Jack Johnson was thrilled by his win over Tommy Burns. Many African Americans shared his joy. Johnson hoped a glorious welcome would be waiting for him in the United States. Unfortunately, there was trouble at home.

News of Johnson's victory thrilled many people. It also angered many people. Sadly, it led to violence in the streets of some American cities. Crowds of Johnson's African-American fans were confronted by mobs of angry whites. Fights broke out. The fights turned into riots, and many people were hurt.

Johnson had hoped to come home as a hero. Instead, he found that many people thought of him as a villain. Most of these people were white. They did not like that an African American had won the championship. They thought whites would always beat African Americans, but Johnson's win proved them wrong.

Whites who did not like Johnson found many things to criticize. They did not like his flashy clothes. They did not approve of his fancy cars, which he loved to drive at high speeds. They did not like the fact that Johnson could not be ignored.

Johnson's place as champion did not free him from the unfairness of **segregation.** His return to North America made that clear. On his first night back, Johnson tried to check into a popular hotel in Victoria, British Columbia, in Canada. But they would not give him a room. The hotel was for whites only.

White Hopes

Promoters and newspaper reporters were looking for a white boxer who could beat the new champ. Johnson defended his championship several times in the year after beating Burns. All of the fights were against white boxers. Promoters tried to convince Jim Jeffries to come back into boxing and take on Johnson. Jeffries had become a farmer after he quit boxing five years earlier. He said he had no interest in getting back into the ring.

The **color line** still made it difficult for an African-American challenger to get a chance, even when the champion was African American. Johnson was under a lot of pressure to take on white opponents. **Promoters** were not interested in letting another African American fight for the title. More tickets could be sold if the fight featured a white challenger against Johnson.

Johnson's Story Retold

Jack Johnson's life story was turned into a smash hit on the stage and screen. A man named Howard Sackler wrote a play based on Johnson's successes and failures. The play was called *The Great White Hope*.

The actor James Earl Jones plays the lead in a movie about Jack Johnson.

The play opened on Broadway in 1969, and audiences loved it. It got rave reviews from critics and won many awards. A movie based on the play was made a short time later. The movie came out in 1970 and was also a success. James Earl Jones, who supplied the voice of Darth Vadar in the *Star Wars* movies, played the lead role. He was nominated for an Academy Award, which is the highest honor for a film actor.

The lead character in both the play and the movie was called Jack Jefferson. But the story was clearly about Johnson. Not everything in Sackler's story was true to life, but it showed many of the challenges Johnson had faced. Sackler said he based his play on a book Johnson wrote to tell his own life story. The book was called *Jack Johnson Is a Dandy*.

Late in 1909, Johnson took on a white fighter named Stanley Ketchel. Ketchel was the middleweight champion and was a very talented boxer. He was much smaller than Johnson, but white fans hoped Ketchel could handle Johnson. They thought Ketchel's boxing skills would make up for the differences in size and strength. Ketchel's fans were in for a surprise.

Johnson was better than Ketchel in every way. Johnson was faster, stronger, and smarter. For 12 rounds, Johnson was in control. He finally knocked out Ketchel with a powerful blow. Many people who were in the crowd said it was the hardest punch ever landed in a boxing match. Ketchel lost the fight.

Fight of the Century

At last, Jim Jeffries agreed to come back to the sport and fight Johnson. People who supported Jeffries still called him the champ. After all, Jeffries was never beaten. He was on top when he left boxing five years earlier. Johnson had dreamed of a fight against Jeffries years earlier. He was thrilled to finally get Jeffries in the ring.

Newspapers said the match would be "The Fight of the Century." Later on, many other great fights would be called by that name, but this one was special. There had never been a sporting event like it before. The fight was scheduled for July 4, 1910, in Reno, Nevada. People across North America and around the world were anxious to see who was the best.

This is a poster for the 1910 World Boxing Championship. It shows Johnson and Jeffries posed, looking ready to fight each other.

Jeffries had been a great champion in earlier years. He spent seven years as a professional boxer. He won the **Heavyweight** Championship for five years in a row. He was admired by millions of boxing fans when he gave up the sport on May 13, 1905. In the following years, Jeffries let himself get out of shape. He had weighed 300 pounds. That was about 100 pounds more than he weighed during his best fighting years. He had a lot of work to do to get ready for the match against Johnson.

Jack Johnson knocks out Jim Jeffries in the 15th round of their famous match on July 4, 1910.

Jeffries looked fit when the day of the fight arrived. He was 35 years old. Johnson was three years younger. The match was scheduled to last 20 rounds. A crowd of more than 20,000 filled a new stadium built for that fight. Most of the crowd were whites who rooted for Jeffries. They would not have much to cheer about.

Johnson had all the glory that day. He wore gray trunks with a U.S. flag tied around his waist like a belt. It was Independence Day, and Johnson was showing his **patriotism**. Even though

Johnson was not accepted by all American people, he continued to stay strong and be patriotic. From the sound of the opening bell, Johnson proved himself to be the better boxer. He moved around the ring gracefully. Jeffries stomped after Johnson but could not catch him. For many rounds, the match moved along without a lot of excitement. Johnson dodged punches and waited for his chance to attack.

The match grew faster and rougher until the 15th round. By then, Jeffries was tired. Johnson seemed to be getting stronger. He went after Jeffries with a series of punches. Jeffries was knocked against the ropes, and Johnson landed another punch. Finally, Jeffries fell to the mat. It was the first time Jeffries had ever been knocked down. He got up to continue fighting. Johnson knocked him down two more times in that round. The fight was stopped to protect Jeffries from injury.

Johnson had won the greatest victory of his career. Again, there was violence in the streets of some American cities following Johnson's win. Crowds of African Americans celebrated Johnson's victory. In some places, angry whites confronted the fans. Celebrations turned into riots. Many people were hurt in street fights and other violence.

Jack Johnson liked fast cars. Here, he poses in a sports car of the day with his manager.

Chapter 5:
Challenges for the Champ

Jack Johnson was riding high after deafeating Jim Jeffries. He lived in Chicago, Illinois, at the time, and that's where he went a few days after his famous victory. A giant crowd of mostly African Americans was waiting for him at the railroad station when he returned from Reno. The fans cheered him, and a marching band played happy tunes. The crowd followed him through the streets from the depot to the house where Johnson's mother lived. The celebration was like a victory parade, although it had not been planned.

Boxing had made Johnson a rich man. He used his money to buy his mother a new home. He also bought himself fancy cars and clothes. He earned more than $100,000 from the match against Jeffries. He expected happy times to come, but again he was faced with many challenges.

Fame and Fortune

At first, Johnson was able to enjoy his fame. He went to New York City later in 1910 and received a hero's welcome. Thousands of fans waited for him to arrive at Grand Central Station, and they cheered when he walked off the train. Many of Johnson's fans were African Americans. Of course, not all of them were. Many whites had been won over by the champ. They admired his skills and were thrilled by his wins. They believed Johnson should be treated fairly in his sport.

Johnson agreed to perform in a **vaudeville** show to earn extra money. That was a kind of stage show that featured singers, dancers, funny skits, and acrobats. Johnson's vaudeville show played in theaters in many cities in the northern states. He told stories, sang, and played the bass on stage. He also showed his boxing skills by **sparring** with a partner. The boxing was just for show. They were not real matches.

Johnson was still the **heavyweight** champion, but he did not box often. Few **contenders** were ready to challenge him at the time. Johnson's next big match did not happen until 1912. The fight was scheduled for July 4 in New Mexico. That was exactly two years after the day Johnson beat Jeffries. This time, he took on Harry Flynn, who was tough and known as a dirty fighter. Johnson knocked Flynn out in the ninth **round.**

Johnson gives a speech at the opening of his new nightclub. His money and fame allowed him to attract people to a place they knew was owned by the champ.

He went back to Chicago and again received a big welcome from fans. Later in 1912, Johnson opened a restaurant in that city. It was called Café de Champion, and it was a popular spot.

Living in Exile

The greatest challenge of Johnson's life began in 1912. Johnson had been charged with a crime that had to do with his relationship with a white woman named Lucille Cameron. Johnson married Lucille on December 4, 1912. Back then, many people did not like African Americans and whites dating. They even passed laws to try to stop it from happening.

They had to leave the United States in 1913 so Johnson could avoid being sent to jail. It was a very difficult thing for him to do. He enjoyed life in the United States, and he wanted to be near his mother. Yet he decided he had to leave.

Johnson and his wife were living in **exile.** To live in exile means to live away from one's home country for a long period of time. Sometimes people are forced into exile. Sometimes they choose to live that way. Johnson and his wife moved first to Paris, France. They lived in several different countries during the next seven years.

It was difficult for Johnson to continue as a boxer when he was in exile. He could not return to the United States for fights.

Jack Johnson's Record in the Ring

Jack Johnson fought more than 100 boxing matches during his career. Most **heavyweights** do not fight nearly so many matches, even a great champion such as Muhammad Ali. In his professional career, Ali fought 61 times.

The International Boxing Hall of Fame lists the following record for Johnson's boxing career:

Won: 77

Lost: 13

Drew: 14

Knockouts: 48

The number of knockouts tells how many of Johnson's wins came by knocking out his opponent. Johnson also boxed in many exhibitions that did not count on his record.

He had to defend his championship in other countries. Johnson had only one serious match in 1913 and one more in 1914. Both matches took place in Paris. Johnson was not in top condition at the time. He found it difficult to practice and train when on the move outside the United States. Johnson kept the championship, but both fights were close calls.

Johnson is weighed before his long fight with Jess Willard.

A New Champion

In 1915, Johnson went to Havana, Cuba, to take on a younger fighter named Jess Willard. Willard was big and strong, but he was not a skilled boxer. Johnson was 37 years old. Although he had lost some of his strength and speed, he was still a better fighter than Jess Willard.

There was something unusual about the match. It was scheduled to last 45 **rounds.** That was a very long fight. The rules in Cuba allowed for longer matches. Johnson was used to the limit being 20 rounds. Today, boxing matches last no more than 12 rounds. The length of the fight probably cost Johnson his championship.

For most of the match, Johnson was in charge. He was too quick for Willard. Johnson dodged Willard's slow attacks. He landed many more punches than Willard did. But the fight dragged on, and Johnson could not knock Willard out.

After the 20th round, Johnson clearly had gotten the best of Willard. If the fight had ended there, the champ would have kept his title. The fight went on, and Johnson soon grew tired. Willard seemed to gain energy. He realized that he had a chance to win and went after Johnson. In the 26th round, Willard landed a series of punches. The last one was a right hand to Johnson's jaw. Johnson fell to the mat and was counted out by the referee.

Willard, a white fighter, was the new heavyweight champion. The next African American to be the champ was Joe Louis, who won the title 22 years later.

Jack Johnson's earnings from boxing allowed him to buy stylish clothes—clothes that many African Americans of the time could not afford .

Chapter 6:
Coming Home

After losing the championship, Jack Johnson had to think about the future. He was 37 years old. Boxing had been his job since he was a teenager. Most boxers would quit the sport by the time they were his age. He did not know what else to do. He wanted to return to the United States, but that seemed impossible. He had many adventures yet to come.

On the Move

The former champ lived in London, England, after he lost to Willard. Johnson began performing for crowds again. He performed at theaters all around England, and fans enjoyed seeing Johnson on stage. His show was called "Seconds Out!" He sang, played his bass, and told stories. He also boxed in short **exhibitions.** An exhibition is just for practice or show. It does not count as a real boxing match.

Johnson decided to leave England in 1916. He moved to Spain and started boxing again. Johnson needed some way to earn money, and boxing was his greatest skill. Many of the fights were exhibitions. He easily beat the men he boxed in Spain. Then he found a different kind of fighting.

Bullfighters are the great heroes of sports fans in Spain. Johnson saw a bullfight and wanted to try it. A local bullfighter showed Johnson how it was done. Soon Johnson was in his first bullfight. He'd never seen an opponent like the bull. It was huge and fast. When it charged at Johnson, one of the bull's horns nicked Johnson's leg. The former champ was able to finish the bullfight without being badly hurt, but it was a close call. He stuck to fighting other people after that.

Johnson stayed in Spain for several years. He wanted to return to the United States to see his mother. She was growing old and her health was not good. Johnson hoped very much he could see her again before she died. He tried to work out a way to see her without having to go to jail. He did not believe he had done anything wrong.

Sadly, Tiny Johnson, the champ's mother, died while he was still in Spain. The bad news was hard on Johnson. His life was sad and difficult then. He finally decided to leave Spain and live in Mexico, closer to the United States where he wanted to be.

Bullfighters try different things to make the bulls charge them. This bullfighter is on his knees, trying to coax the bull to charge. When the bull charges, the bullfighter will get out of the way at the last second.

Back in the U.S.A.

Johnson began boxing often in Mexico. He said he wanted a chance to be heavyweight champion again. In 1919, Jack Dempsey had won the championship. He knocked out Jess Willard, who had beaten Johnson back in 1915. Many people said Dempsey was one of the greatest boxers ever. Johnson wanted a chance to show that he was even better.

Johnson won five matches in 1919 and had one draw. He won twice more in the first part of 1920. The fights were held in Mexico and were against fighters of little fame or talent. Johnson wanted to show he was still a top boxer. He was living in a city called Tijuana at the time. It is near the border of the United States. Johnson opened a restaurant there, as he had done back in Chicago. It looked like he might be in Mexico for good.

One day in July 1920, Johnson did something that surprised many people. He went to the U.S. border and told the guards he wanted to go home. That meant Johnson would have to go to prison. A judge had ruled that Johnson had to spend one year and one day in prison. Johnson decided it was worth it. He wanted to live the rest of his life in his home country. He went to prison even though he did not believe he had done anything wrong. The U.S. government sent Johnson to a prison in Leavenworth, Kansas. Johnson was surprised at how well he was treated there.

Jack Johnson gives himself up for arrest to a California sheriff at the border between Mexico and the United States.

Muhammed Ali talks to reporters in his usual outspoken way at a press conference in London. Ali saw Jack Johnson as a role model.

At Leavenworth, the man who ran the prison was a fan of Johnson's. He put Johnson in charge of gym programs for the other prisoners. He also set up boxing matches in the prison yard. Johnson fought six times during his time in prison. He won every match.

He was released from prison early because of his good behavior. By July 1921, Johnson was a free man in his homeland. He found that things had changed since he left the United States in 1913.

He had fans everywhere. Many people who once disliked him had changed their minds. The former champ was more popular than ever.

Muhammad Ali

Jack Johnson became a hero to many African-American boxers who came later. He opened the door for other African-American champs when other sports remained for whites only. He also had a style and personality like few other people.

Muhammad Ali was one fighter who admired Johnson. Born in 1942, Ali was the heavyweight champion in the 1960s and 1970s. Like Johnson, Ali was also famous for his personality. He was outgoing and funny. He loved to talk. Sometimes, things he said made people angry. Many people think Ali was the greatest boxer ever to live, and Jack Johnson was Ali's role model.

In 1970, Ali was getting ready for a big fight against a boxer named Jerry Quarry. Ali watched an old film the night before the match. The film showed Jack Johnson at his best. He was taking on Tommy Burns for the championship. Johnson was awesome. At the end of one round, Johnson waved goodbye to Burns. It was Johnson's way of showing that it was over for Burns. Ali was impressed.
He went out the next night and knocked out Quarry.

Jack Johnson acted in an opera called Aida *in New York City in 1936. Acting was one of the things that his fame allowed him the opportunity to try.*

Chapter 7: Johnson's Place in History

Jack Johnson lived out the rest of his years in the United States. His fame was lasting. He always found a way to entertain fans. Sometimes he was in the boxing ring. Sometimes he was on a stage. It didn't matter where he was. Johnson thrilled people.

For many years, Johnson did a show in New York City. He told stories about his life. He talked about his childhood back in Galveston, Texas. He told exciting stories about his many boxing matches. He explained what it was like to be the first African-American **heavyweight** champion. He talked about his adventures around the world. Thousands of people of all races went to the show.

Johnson had a message about **racism**. Racism is the idea that one race is superior to another. Johnson told people to be color blind. That meant people should not pay attention to the color of a person's skin. Johnson thought people should be judged by what they can do, not what they look like.

A Tragic Accident

In 1946, Johnson was driving from Texas to New York. He was passing through North Carolina on June 10. He lost control of his car. It went off the road and hit a light pole. The former champion was rushed to a hospital in Raleigh, North Carolina. The doctors could not save him. He was 68 years old.

Johnson was driving too fast that day in North Carolina. He was rushing to see a boxing match involving Joe Louis. Louis was the second African American to be **heavyweight** champion. Since Johnson's death, many other African Americans have become champions in boxing.

One year later, Jackie Robinson broke through the **color line** in baseball. He was the first African American to play in the major leagues. He was a star. Soon many other African Americans were playing for professional baseball teams all around the country. Sports became a place where people were treated equally. They were judged by what they could do on the field, not by the color of their skin.

A Hero in History

Jack Johnson's name lives on in boxing. He opened a door for other African-American athletes. He is remembered by many people as a great champion. His skill at dodging and blocking punches has never been topped. Johnson's fame lasted longer than his life. In

Jack Johnson poses for the camera in 1945, a year before his death.

Johnson, right, advises a young boxer named Leroy Haynes. Later in life and after his death, Johnson became an inspiration to many African-American boxers.

the late 1960s, people were still interested in him. In fact, Johnson was probably more popular then than he had been when he was the champion. A play based on Johnson's life had become a hit in 1969. It was called *The Great White Hope*. The play showed Johnson as a hero who battled against **racism.** That play was made into a movie, which also became a hit. Millions of people went to see the movie and learned about the first African-American heavyweight champion.

The End of a Long Journey

Jack Johnson was famous around the world. He boxed in North America, South America, Australia, and Europe. He lived away from the United States for seven years. In 1990, Johnson was named to the International Boxing Hall of Fame in Canastota, New York. However, what he did was more important than where he went or how famous he was.

Johnson believed he could be champion when that seemed impossible. No African American had ever been given the chance. The **color line** was in the way. Johnson won a fight against racism. That was a greater win than anything he ever did in the ring.

Glossary

aggressive   threatening way of behaving

color line   name for a barrier in society that limits the rights of people of color

contender   boxer who is ranked in the top 10 in his weight group and is ready for a chance at the championship

draw   tie in boxing. If a match is even when all rounds have been fought, neither boxer is awarded a victory.

exhibition   demonstration. In boxing, an exhibition is a match done just for practice or show. It does not count on the records of the boxers.

exile   to live away from one's home country for a long period of time

heavyweight   group of boxers that weigh the most. Heavyweights normally compete against other heavyweights. Sometimes they fight against boxers in other weight groups, such as middleweights.

patriotism   love and loyalty for a country

promoter   person who organizes boxing matches. Promoters sell the tickets to the public and pay the fighters.

racism   idea that one race is superior to another

round   period during which boxers compete. Each round lasts three minutes. Boxers rest for one minute between rounds. The number of rounds in a boxing match varies.

segregation   rules or laws that force groups of people to live apart from each other

sparring   practice boxing with few heavy punches. A sparring partner is someone a professional boxer fights for practice.

vaudeville   stage show that featured singers, dancers, funny skits, and acrobats. Vaudeville shows were popular during the first part of the 1900s.

Timeline

1878 – Johnson is born in Galveston, Texas.

1890 – Johnson leaves school after fifth grade and goes to work.

1897 – Johnson wins his first professional boxing match.

1899 – Johnson loses for the first time as a professional.

1900 – Flood hits Galveston and destroys the home of Johnson's parents.

1902 – Johnson beats Jack Jeffries, the brother of the white **heavyweight** champ.

1903 – Johnson wins the Colored Heavyweight Champion of the World.

1908 – Johnson defeats Tommy Burns and becomes the first African American to be heavyweight champion.

1910 – Johnson defeats former champ Jim Jeffries.

1913 – Johnson leaves the United States and begins to live in **exile.**

1914 – Johnson lives in Paris, France, and defends his championship in matches there.

1915 – Johnson loses the heavyweight championship in Havana, Cuba.

1916 – Johnson moves to Spain. He tries bullfighting there.

1919 – Johnson boxes in Mexico. He hopes to make a comeback and fight champion Jack Dempsey. He never gets that chance.

1920 – Johnson returns to the United States and is sent to prison in Leavenworth, Kansas.

1921 – Johnson is released from prison early.

1945 – Johnson boxes for the last time at age 67. He participates in a three-round exhibition in New York City.

1946 – Johnson dies after a car accident in North Carolina.

Further Information

Further reading

Jakoubek, Robert. *Jack Johnson: Heavyweight Champion.* Broomall, Penn.: Chelsea House, 1990.

Knapp, Ron. *Top 10 Heavyweight Boxers.* Springfield, N.J.: Enslow Publishers, 1997.

Potter, Jean, and Constance Clayton. *African Americans Who Were First.* New York: Coblehill Books, 1997.

Addresses

Smithsonian Anacostia Museum &
Center for African American Culture
1901 Fort Place SE
Washington, DC 20020

National Association for the
Advancement of Colored People
4805 Mount Hope Drive
Baltimore, MD 21215

International Boxing Hall of Fame
1 Hall of Fame Drive
Canastota, NY 13032

Institute for African American
Studies
312 Holmes
Hunter Academic Building
University of Georgia
Athens, GA 30602

Index